Baby & A Blonde

A MODERN MOTHER'S JOURNEY

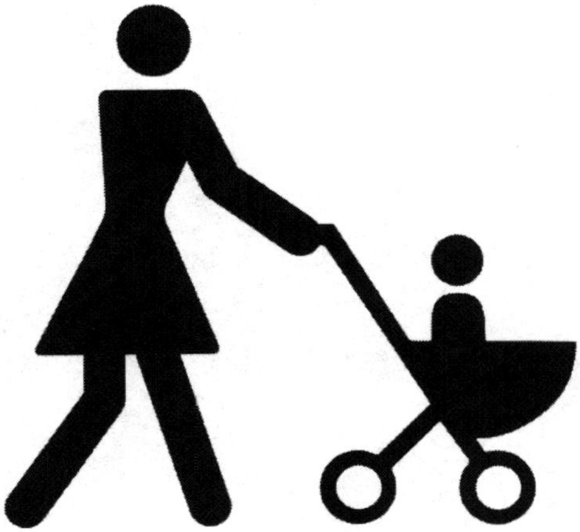

Victoria Wells

Baby & A Blonde

A Modern Mother's Journey

Copyright Victoria Wells 2016

The right of Victoria Wells to be identified as the author of this work has been asserted in accordance with the Copyright, Designs and Patents Act 1988.

This book was first published in Great Britain in 2016 by Victoria Wells.

All rights reserved. Apart from any permitted use under UK copyright law, this publication may only be reproduced, stored or transmitted, in any form, or by any means, with prior permission in writing of the publisher or, in the case of reprographic production, in accordance with the terms of licenses issued by the Copyright Licensing Agency.

ISBN: 978-1-5262-0269-7

Printed and bound in the UK by 4 Edge Limited

Every effort has been made to ensure the information in this book is accurate. However, it is not intended to be a substitute for the advice of your doctor or health care professional. Neither the publisher nor the author accepts any legal responsibility for any personal injury or other damage or loss arising from the use or misuse of the information and advice in this book.

Every effort has been made to fulfil requirements with regard to reproducing copyright material. The author and the publisher will be glad to rectify any omissions at the earliest opportunity.

For all first time mothers. x

CONTENTS

Introduction 13

BEAUTY 20
Face Intro 21 | Skin Types 25 | Products 27 | Routines 34 | Breakouts & Pigmentation 40 | Antioxidants 44 | Beauty Weapons 50 | Make Up 53 | Hair 55 | Online Stockists 60

BODY 62
How I Got My Figure Back 64 | Bodily Changes 69 | Stretch Marks & Scars 71 | Skin Maintenance 72 | Fitness 76 | Workouts 83 | Social Media 88 | Body shapes 89

MIND 100
The Mind 103 | Support Network & Communication 107 | How To Not Lose Your Sh*t 110 | Boredom 112 | Baby Brain 115 | Your Space 116

A Final Word 120
Thank You's 123

INTRODUCTION

I wrote this book to share my journey as a first time mother. How I went from looking and feeling terrible post-birth to finding myself feeling and looking healthy, happy and better than ever.

Obviously, my priority is being a mother. However, part of being a successful mother is looking after yourself.

The three areas I wanted to focus on post-birth were Beauty, Body and Mind.

Beauty was an important area because I wanted to look better, have glowing and radiant skin, healthy hair and feel confident about myself and how I looked.
Body was important because I wanted to slim down, learn how to look after my body, become stronger, leaner and overall, healthier.
Mind was important because having a baby really turned my world upside down - I didn't know what had hit me and mentally, it took a toll on me, so I really wanted to understand how to cope with that.

I want this book to make you smile and give you hope that bouncing back after a baby isn't as daunting, stressful and difficult as some people make out.

It should be an enjoyable experience but I know what you're thinking - how are all these things possible with a newborn? Well, they **are**.

When we welcome a baby into the world, everything changes - that's it; it changes... it doesn't disappear. All of a sudden, you find you have no spare time. Things you previously enjoyed doing, you rarely get to do. Even the simplest of pre baby habits like eating well, taking care of your appearance or reading a book are an effort.

Whilst having a baby is probably one of, if not, THE greatest feelings in the universe, the excitement can be short-lived. Once home from hospital, your life is thrown into all-consuming disarray and you soon find there is very little time for you.

It is hard to divide your time between baby, yourself and those around you - but it is possible. Trust me.

I'm sure there are women out there who can relate to my journey.

This book isn't a smug tome nor am I writing a lengthy health practitioner's manual. But what I can tell you is that this book has been written as a reflection of honest experiences from my perspective as a real world first time mother. I hope you find it helpful, interesting and a little amusing too.

Everything in this book, I have learnt or researched along the way and experienced for myself through trial and error. I have spent hours researching products, reading blogs, stalking online beauty experts, trying out products and new fitness regimes. I have devoted all my spare time over the last year to this book.

When we look better, we automatically feel better. It's not always that simple to leave the house with a child looking pristine but for the sake of our self-esteem and confidence of all mothers, we sure as hell can give it a go!

Everyone loves to see a yummy mummy - if anything, it gives future mums hope! Be an inspiration to others.

From one new mother to another, I hope this book helps you in some way. Whether it's taking care of your skin, feeling more confident about yourself, dressing better, exercising more at home or simply feeling confident and happy, well thats just hunky dory.

Before we get started and so you know that I am not a robot, I'm going to paint my post-birth picture for you...

I felt ugly, fat and disgusting. None of my clothes would fit, everything was clinging to me awkwardly. I had acne across most of my upper body and my face was so bloated I looked like I had just had dental surgery. My stomach was podgy, sore and held together by a beige girdle. I had a premature newborn in intensive care, one boob bigger than the other and bad, bad roots!

I tried so hard in the first few months not let my appearance get me down, but it did. My confidence plummeted. I saw so many other mothers who just seemed to know instinctively what they were doing but not only that, looking incredible whilst effortlessly pushing their strollers along, skinny coffee in one hand, baby wipes discreetly in the other. They looked toned, healthy and happy. I longed to be that person. I felt miserable and disgusting. I remember I used to get so upset and would just cry and moan at my husband and expect him magically to wave a wand so I could go back to my former self and body.

Looking back on it now, I appreciate how bloody ridiculous I must have seemed. But on reflection, I now know that it was the biological inevitability of becoming a first time mother - the combination of shock and hormones!

On one occasion I decided I wanted to wear a pair of jeans ... Imagine a crazy woman trying to squeeze a size 14 ass into a pair of size 10 jeans.... how my husband didn't laugh in my face genuinely amazes me.

Aside from my junk in the trunk issues and leaking breasts (yep, sexy!), my skin was terrible, I felt rubbish and my hair was dull, limp and lifeless. I was drinking mostly smoothies or eating chocolate whenever I needed that sugar hit/energy boost. I wasn't finding being a mother easy at all. My emotions were binary one week, ecstatic the next. I was all over the place! One day I decided that enough was enough! Any of this sound familiar?!

I needed an overhaul! I wanted to sort myself out - physically and mentally - for the sake of myself, my marriage and my child.

I didn't need to seek out my motivation, it was staring me in the face. My husband. I wanted to impress my husband and still do.

Find your motivation and stick to it!

(Please note: all views that follow are my own!)

1
BEAUTY

Before I had a baby I spent a lot of time trying to look good. I would always wear make up, nice clothes and was extremely sociable. I didn't eat particularly well or get nearly enough decent sleep or rest. I had the occasional cigarette and drank far too much. In turn, my skin wasn't great but I didn't care - I just covered it up with make up! There were times when I didn't even remove make up after a big night, I would just fall into bed. I didn't take much notice of my figure nor was I overly bothered about being fit or healthy. I was in my 20s and figured my body would just look after itself.

How wrong I was!

I'm going to run through a few beauty basics with you in this section. You'd be amazed at how many women don't know or understand the beauty basics. I for one only learnt all of this a year or so ago and now want to preach it to everyone because quite frankly it has really saved the skin on my face and body!

Beauty as a confidence builder is a major part of any female's life, regardless of sexual orientation or life choices. The foundation to our beauty is our skin so it is important to make sure we understand it and use the correct products & techniques. Even if you only have a spare 10 minutes a day, you can still look after your skin, keep it clean and prevent quicker ageing.

I had shocking skin as a teenager, which continued throughout my 20s. It got particularly bad again during the first trimester of my pregnancy. I had acne all over my forehead and nothing would help it vanish. I certainly didn't get 'the glow'!

Since having a child I have taken much better care of my skin - I think my pregnancy acne traumatised me! Needless to say, I have learned a lot about skincare and products along the way. I hope you find some of the information in this section/chapter useful and if you are suffering with bad skin, please don't panic!

One of the biggest mistakes everyone tends to make with skincare is using the wrong products for their skin type or lacking routine (using the products in the wrong order).

Now, by no means is my skin perfect but I have finally learnt what my bad skin triggers are:
- Poor diet/heavy sugar foods
- Badly cleansed skin
- Thick/rich creams.

So now I can control these triggers by avoiding them. I also suffer from PCOS which means I can occasionally get breakouts along my jawline and neck. Again, keeping my skin really clean has helped with this.

You're going to think I'm completely OCD but I have my weekly skincare routine ritual written on my bathroom mirror!

Top Tip - Use a dry wipe marker to write reminders where you can't miss them! Alternatively, its also a great way to use up old and disgustingly coloured lipsticks!

So, lets get to it. **B E A U T Y**. Your long lost friend is about to come storming back into your life with a vengeance! (sorry, I got a little carried away there)

A few basic rules before we get started:

✦Always cleanse morning and evening and always remove make up!

✦If you don't remove make up it enlarges the pores and this can lead to inflammation and breakouts due to excessive dirt and grease left in the pores from make up.

✦**NEVER** sleep with your make up on or with dirty skin. Even if you're shattered, thirty seconds to wash your face is better than the next morning's results - YUK

SKIN TYPES

There are five basic skin types, however it is possible to be more than one type. It is important to know your own skin type to help determine the type of products you use.

1 - Normal

- Characterised by hardly any pores or imperfections with an overall natural glow.

2 - Dry

- Characterised by dull, flaky skin with a rough texture and dry to touch.

3 - Sensitive

- General signs are irritation, red patches, dryness and regular breakouts.

4 - Oily

- Characterised by enlarged pores, shine, and prone to breakouts.

5 - Combination

A mixture of all the other skin types: oily on the t-zone, dry and sometimes sensitive elsewhere.

"Looking after your skin in the short term will help to ensure beautiful glowing and radiant skin in the long term"

PRODUCTS - WHICH, HOW AND WHEN

✦ Cleanser

What does it do? Simply put, it washes (cleanses) your face.

This should take a few minutes to do. Take time to really rub in the cleanser and let it do its thing. It cannot remove dirt and make up if it's only on your face for a nano second.

Remember to distribute cleanser equally all over the face and under the chin and jaw line. Make sure you reach those outer edges but be gentle; don't try and scrub your skin off! Remove with either warm water or a flannel.

Types of cleanser include creams, foams, exfoliating cleanser and oil based cleansers. If you use cleanser both morning and night everyday, you will notice a wonderful difference to your skin.

Little note: if you have been sweating (chasing after your children or exercising), make sure you wash your face as soon as possible to avoid the sweat and dirt settling into your open pores.

✦Serum

What does it do?

Serum absorbs deep into the skin, targeting the dermis. There are various serums available and all are directed at various aspects of skincare - hydration, brightness, rejuvenation, targeting the signs of ageing, etc... Serum is applied before your moisturiser.

Serums are highly concentrated and active. This means that they need to be applied first to treat the skin, ensuring all the active ingredients can penetrate your skin.
These active ingredients are the reason why serums are more expensive than regular moisturisers. The high concentrations in the raw materials push the price up.

Remember that not all serums will work with all moisturisers. If you are unsure, either use serums and moisturisers from the same brand, or check the serum to see if it says that if can be included in your normal beauty routine, or if it's a standalone product.

Ideally, you should invest in a quality serum with peptides or antioxidants and layer it under a hydrating night cream to seal the moisture. Apply these powerful anti-ageing ingredients at night because that's when the skin starts to regenerate and repair itself.

How to apply serum correctly:

✦ Apply tiny dots of serum all over your cleansed moist face and then blend quickly & lightly all over.

✦ Use light but firm strokes to apply your face serum. Do not stretch, pull or rub your skin.

✦ After applying and whilst the serum is still wet, tap the surface of your face with your fingers for half a minute. You can use all your fingers both hands on either side of your face very lightly. The tapping action encourages the serum to sink, penetrating the epidermis as far as is able.

- If you feel any tingling sensations when you apply the serum – don't worry. Tingling can be a sign the active ingredients in the serum are penetrating and reaching the dermis – where they need to be if they are going to work. I've personally seen the best results for serum ingredients including vitamin C and retinoids

- Only when your serum is fully dry (touch dry on your face), which should take around 3 minutes, should you apply your oils and moisturisers

Top Tip: Proper layering is key to quicker results. When you layer a serum underneath a cream, the serum should penetrate deeper into the skin.

✦ Moisturiser

What does it do?

Moisturisers help to keep skin hydrated. However, there are several types of moisturisers available all of which work in different ways. Do your research before you buy! The moisturiser you choose will be suited to your own personal needs. For example, I need an SPF, oil-free, hydrating day moisturiser for my oily skin.

Day moisturisers tend to be quite light. Make sure it has SPF to help avoid sun damage. If you are a sun worshipper thats fine, you can still tan through SPF!

Night-time creams tend to be richer and thicker, therefore don't need to be applied as liberally. A good night-time alternative is facial oil; it's lighter on the skin but just as beneficial.

How to Apply Moisturiser

- Pump a pea size dollop of moisturiser into the palm of your hand.

- Rub your palms together, warming up the moisturiser and spreading it between your palms.

- Start with your cheeks (as they are drier) and then spread the moisturiser gently to your forehead, nose and lastly the chin.

- The T-zone and chin will usually be a little oilier so you don't need to apply as much moisturiser as compared to your cheeks.

- Alternatively, if you've been a little generous with your allocation, apply any remaining moisturiser to your hands and forearms.

I can empathise that when you have a baby, the last thing you want to do is start putting several lotions and potions on your face before bed. You just want to hit the pillow.
I completely understand! But please please try to be disciplined with a solid night-time routine - it will pay off in future years. Also, the aroma of some oils may help you to sleep, especially if you find one with lavender in it.

Another reason I love my night routine is because it's a little bit of me pamper time. I get to spend a few minutes enjoying some peace and quiet whilst enjoying lovely skincare products. I light a candle and just relax for a bit whilst applying everything. (Obviously keep the candle away from the products!) Then I can go to bed feeling calm and relaxed. (MOST OF THE TIME!)

QUICK & EASY DAILY SKINCARE ROUTINES

A general rule of thumb when apply skincare products is always thinnest to thickest – the thinner the consistency, the earlier you need to apply it.

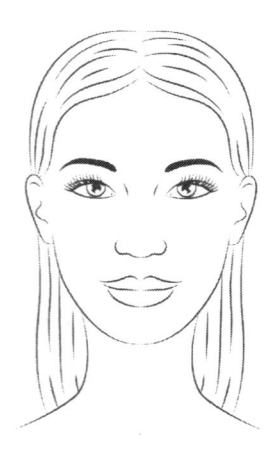

So basically, after cleansing, apply serums, then oils, then gels and finally creams, always applying sun protection last. Make sure to leave a few minutes between each application for the products to absorb.

✦ Morning Cleansing Routine

Of course, everyone's routine is different. My daily routine is quick and effective and helps to achieve and maintain healthy and glowing skin.

1. Apply cleansing face wash to dry skin. Gently rub all over the face and jaw line for a minute then rinse with lukewarm water. (Don't use scorching hot water, not only will it really hurt but it also will damage your skin!)

2. Apply a small amount of exfoliator and gently rub over the face for 30 seconds. Rinse with water. Please don't try to scrub your skin off, gently does it!

3. Apply a couple of drops of rejuvenating serum and gently press over face.

4. Apply hydrating (oil free) SPF moisturiser and a dab of balm to my lips.

◆ Night Time Cleansing Routine

1. Apply cleansing face wash to skin. (Same as step 1 from morning routine.)

2. Remove any traces of eye make up (if you have been wearing any) with remover.

3. Apply oil-based cleanser and massage around face then wash off with luke warm water - this is so you get every scrap of make up or dirt off the skin.

4. Apply night serum - same as step 3 from morning routine.

5. Massage a pea sized amount of night cream onto face and another dab of lip balm.

Every other night I apply either facial oil instead of moisturiser or leave my skin to breathe.

Little note: cleansing at night is not just about unclogging pores. During the day, pollution particles attach themselves to our foundation, and to creams. No matter how tired you are, if you don't wash it all off before you go to bed at night, you're fighting that extra free-radical damage all night long, and pollution, which has been shown to cause brown spots and sun spots.

A NOTE ON EXFOLIATION

Exfoliation removes dead skin cells and helps the skin reproduce new healthy ones. It keeps the face looking bright, young and feeling very smooth.

Exfoliation is NOT scrubbing! It should be done very gently. The red, raw face is not a look we are going for....ever!

Try and gently exfoliate your face everyday.

"Cleansing can be so quick, easy and effective when done correctly."

MONEY ISN'T ALWAYS THE ANSWER

You can have the most expensive products available, but if used incorrectly, they are a complete waste of money and time. Take time to research products. What works with your skin type? Which products are within your budget? Are they good value? Is there enough to last you a while?

You don't need a massive budget in order to maintain beautiful looking skin - you just need to understand how and when to use products. Once you've got that, you will be desperate to try so many of the different products that are available today.

BREAKOUTS & PIGMENTATION

Everyone gets the odd spot, breakout or overall angry and stressed out looking skin. There are no quick fixes unfortunately to get rid of breakouts. However, the good news is you can try to avoid the following to help prevent further breakouts:

- ✦ Greasy food
- ✦ Refined (white) sugar
- ✦ Not cleaning your face properly
- ✦ Unnecessary Stress
- ✦ Some Medicines
- ✦ Dirt & free radicals

"DO NOT PICK THOSE SPOTS!"

BREAKOUTS DO'S & DONT'S

✦ Don't start picking at a pimple. Leave it alone!

✦ Do keep your skin as clean as possible

✦ Don't squeeze it, you'll damage the skin around the pimple.

✦ Don't worry - everyone gets them!

✦ Do amend your diet or lifestyle if breakouts are a frequent occurrence.

✦ Do let your skin breathe

✦ Do stay hydrated as much as possible

✦ Don't skip your sleep - this is when our skin repairs itself

✦ Don't cake your face in products that aren't suited to your skin type - this can upset your skin and lead to breakouts or reactions

POST BIRTH BREAKOUTS

My skin post-birth was terrible. I think the combination of drugs from hospital, the stress of my baby being premature, hormonal changes and tiredness all contributed to my horrendous breakouts.

We are all quick to forget that our bodies go through tremendous change, stress and trauma throughout pregnancy and birth - this all takes its toll on your body but especially on your skin.

If you are suffering with post baby skin problems or acne, be as caring and gentle with your skin as you are with your baby's - use only mild products. Remember to keep your skin as clean as possible, and ensure you cleanse twice a day.

It will clear up with time. Be patient.

PIGMENTATION

Such an awful word!

I know many women whose pregnancies have led to them getting small darkened patches on their faces. This is very common in pregnancy and is called Chloasma (getting technical now).

This change in pigmentation on the face is caused by the high level of pregnancy hormones in your body. As the hormones decrease post birth, the darkened patches will become less obvious and should gradually fade in the year after birth.

Don't panic! Try to keep your face out of the sun (UV light will make it darker) and use skin tone correcting moisturisers or speak to a dermatologist for a more in depth solution.

ANTIOXIDANTS

Antioxidants can be really confusing and daunting. Which one does what and how do I incorporate it into my routine?! I never used to even think twice about antioxidants - I always thought they were just silly marketing gimmicks... but they're not.

There are so many benefits to using antioxidants. Lets have a little look at some of the benefits:

✦ Combat the free-radical damage that is responsible for the visible (and hidden) signs of ageing

✦ Enhance the effectiveness of sunscreens in preventing sun damage. During the day, the combination of antioxidants plus sun protection is a strong defence against many signs of ageing, including wrinkles, dullness, and discolouration.

✦ Using antioxidants at night will promote cellular repair and healing.

Which Antioxidants are Best?

There are hundreds of trendy antioxidants that show up in so many skin-care lines, but antioxidants don't need to be exotic or have a good marketing story to work brilliantly.

When planning to treat your skin to a variety of antioxidants, compare it to drinking cocktails (oh those happy days!) This cocktail approach gives your skin its very own happy hour with an array of potent, stable and well-researched antioxidants!

Your skin gets the most benefit when several antioxidants are applied together, very similar to how eating a variety of fruits and vegetables is healthier than eating only apples or only broccoli.

Here are a few effective antioxidants, and how to get the most out of them in your skin-care routine.

◆Vitamin E
One of the most well-known antioxidants, Vit E is a fat-soluble antioxidant and provides well documented benefits for your skin.

Vit E works to protect cell membranes from oxidative damage and from the early stages of ultraviolet light damage. It also works in powerful synergy with Vitamin C so a serum or treatment that contains both vitamins C and E can be doubly beneficial.

◆Vitamin C
Vitamin C is a potent antioxidant that works particularly well for treating wrinkles, dullness and brown spots. It is considered an anti-ageing superstar.

Note that Vit C, like any antioxidant, must be packaged to protect it from excess exposure to light and air

Vitamin C has been proven to increase collagen production, including dermal collagen, which is significant in the fight against wrinkles. There is also research showing that Vit C reduces skin discolourations, strengthens the skin's barrier response, enhances the skin's repair process, reduces inflammation, and helps skin better withstand exposure to sunlight. Vit C is found in all sorts of products, from lip balms to eye creams, but you'll get the most out of this antioxidant in targeted treatment products and skin-brightening serums.

◆Resveratrol
Resveratrol is a potent polyphenolic antioxidant that's found in red grapes, red wine (great news!), nuts and fruits such as blueberries and cranberries.

Resveratrol has incredible protective benefits for the skin. It protects against sun damage, improves collagen production and reduces cell damage. It also has significant anti-inflammatory properties. Look for resveratrol in moisturizers and anti-ageing makeup.

◆Retinol
This is the the term given to the entire Vitamin A molecule, which has a long-established reputation as a brilliant ingredient for skin. It provides multiple benefits when used on a regular basis. Although it is not the only ingredient to look for in an anti-ageing product, it deserves strong consideration by anyone who

wants to keep their skin younger and healthier over the years. An added benefit is that retinol also has been shown to reduce breakouts, brown spots and red marks from past breakouts.

Retinol helps skin create better, healthier skin cells and increase the production of skin-support substances such as ceramides. Retinol has been shown to increase the skin's collagen production resulting in firmer skin with improved texture. If you want firmer skin, use retinol! Retinol is found in all types of products, from moisturizers to serums, to body treatments and many others.

Top Tip: new research shows that retinol is helpful for those with rosacea (redness/sensitive skin) because it works against the inflammation that causes the persistent redness.

"Healthy, hydrated cells are the key to ageless skin and a healthy body."

BEAUTY WEAPONS

Here are a few little beauty weapons that have been tried and tested by myself and friends.

- Sudacrem - did you know that miracle baby bottom cream is also a secret weapon for breakouts on the face? The healing and antiseptic properties help to heal and soothe the affected areas.

- Epsom salts - when dissolved in warm water are easily absorbed through the skin where they immediately go to work inside our bodies. They relieve stress by heightening serotonin levels and reducing the negative effects of adrenaline. This helps us to feel invigorated without feelings of restlessness or anxiety.

- Aztec Secret Indian Healing Clay - an incredible face mask. It contains 100% natural calcium bentonite clay which targets deep pores. Labelled the 'worlds most powerful facial', it can be mixed with either water or apple cider vinegar for epic results.

✦Nipple balm - also works amazingly well as a lip balm! If you have any left over from your breastfeeding days, save it!

✦Coconut water - try to drink a glass a day. It is super hydrating which contributes to healthy glowing skin.

✦Ice cubes - if you want to switch up your night time routine, rub an ice cube all over your face before bed. It tightens the pores and leaves your face feeling really firm

✦Anti-oxidants - if you don't want to rub them into your face, add them to your diet! They're found in so many super foods such as blueberries, red berries, dark grapes, beans, nuts and green tea.

✦Rose water spray - a great alternative to toner. It refreshes your skin, balances it out and wakes you up, not to mention smelling of beautiful roes! Win, win!

✦Sunglasses - buy a decent pair! Every time you squint into sunlight, you're creating wrinkles around the eyes, just by making the movement repeatedly. The other reason is because the skin around the eyes is very thin and very fragile, so it's especially prone to damage from UV rays.

✦ Green Tea - research has shown that coffee protects against skin cancer, but green tea is actually better for anti-ageing. If you can alternate every cup of coffee with a cup of green tea, you're actually getting more powerful antioxidants that way—and the green tea slows down the degradation of collagen.

MAKE UP

My mother has always told me to try and leave the house with a bit of make up on - not only will it make you feel better about yourself and how you look but it's also about taking pride in your appearance, even when you are exhausted!

If you look good, you will automatically feel better about yourself. This has always applied to me, pre and post pregnancy. You don't need to leave the house caked in it, but a little make up helps give us that spring in our step!

> "Make up shouldn't hide your features, it should enhance them."

Here are a few daily essentials to help you on your way with a quick & easy make up routine

✦Tinted moisturiser or cc cream
✦Good light concealer for under the eyes. Get a slightly lighter colour for under the eyes as you want the light to enhance the eyes
✦Eyeshadow - a natural tone coloured eyeshadow is a must have. Or use a bronzer as an eyeshadow. Incredibly flattering on most women and easy to apply with a natural effect on the eye
✦Mascara - use a wearable lasting non crumbling one
✦White eyeliner trick on water line. Brightens the eyes
✦Blush - pop a little colour on the cheeks and you are good to go
✦Bronzer - apply to the hollows of the face if needed, temples and jawline
✦Lips - always need a little balm. After all, you are likely to be showering your child with kisses so lipstick is probably best to be avoided during the daytime!

HAIR

During pregnancy you may have been thrilled with your thick, lustrous and healthy mane of hair. You may have been pleasantly surprised how pregnancy had finally given your hair some life! I know I was! However, once you have your baby - BOOM! It's a shock to discover that your hair seems to be falling out. (which really sucks). This is very normal and happens to the majority of new mums so don't worry.

Let's go into this in a little more detail - this hair loss is a temporary phase so don't panic. In the normal cycle of hair growth, some hair is lost every day. However, during pregnancy the increased levels of oestrogen in your body freezes hair in the growing or "resting" phase of the cycle. Hair that would normally fall out stays put, resulting in thicker hair. After you give birth and your oestrogen levels decline, all that hair that was resting starts to fall out. This usually starts on the third or fourth postpartum and ends by six months, however some women say it can last for a year.

This temporary hair loss doesn't mean you're deficient in nutrition or vitamins. It's simply hormonal.

Sometimes hair falls out all over your head. Or clumps may come out when you brush it or even in the shower. Often women just lose a lot around their hairline, so that their hair looks very thin in the front or as if they're going bald. Not nice. It will grow back - don't panic!

I lost quite a bit of hair along my hairline which lasted around 8 months. It has now finally started to grow back and now i have these 'wisps'. Luckily my son has matching wisps from his lack of hair growth so we look quite cute together now with our wisps!

LITTLE NOTE ON MAINTENANCE

Thoroughly shampooing and conditioning your hair as needed, will aid recovery and growth. Try and use a deep conditioning mask 2-3 times a week. Don't use excess heat tools on your hair especially round the face area on the wisps and if blow drying use protecting heat products accordingly.

DAILY HAIRSTYLES

If you have suffered postpartum hair loss, do not try and start experimenting with overly glamorous and complex daily hairstyles!
If styling, try to style it so your lack of hair is hidden or similarly, try to hide the wisps. Don't scrape your hair back from your face if you are conscious about these little stray bits of hair. Brush them back with a toothbrush and set with hair spray if you must wear it up.

Personally, I try to let my hair air dry most days as it is naturally curly (messy) and pray that my wisps just blend in with the rest of my beach/bed hair! (I still have wisps 13 months on...!)

HANDY HOME TREATMENTS

There are a couple of handy home treatments - Cover your hair in either coconut oil or aargan oil, wrap in a towel and leave on over night. If your budget is higher, use a deep-conditioning treatment and leave on your hair for 2-3 hours.

Don't stress about the wisps and stay positive! Remember it is normal and eventually everything will grow back. Avoid heating your hair without full heat protection as the wisps are delicate and could break easily. Look after them!

TOP TIPS

◆Pick a hairstyle that is manageable!

◆If you are in a rush, wear a hat

◆Avoid overheating your hair

◆Be gentle when brushing it

◆Brush wisps back with a toothbrush

◆Use hair spray to hide wisps

Online Beauty Stockists

- Feel Unique - www.feelunique.com
- Space NK - www.spacenk.com
- Boots - www.boots.com
- StrawberryNet - www.strawberrynet.com
- Net A Porter - www.net-a-porter.com
- Sephora - www.sephora.com
- Get the gloss - www.getthegloss.com
- Beauty Mart - www.thisisbeautymart.com
- Love Lula - www.lovelula.com
- Cult Beauty - www.cultbeauty.co.uk
- Victoria Health - www.victoriahealth.com
- Beauty Bay - www.beautybay.com
- Look Fantastic - www.lookfantastic.com
- Being Content - www.beingcontent.com
- My Showcase - www.myshowcase.com

2
BODY

I cannot even begin to tell you how much I worried about my body, the size of it, and if it was ever going to look or feel the same again. I only realised post birth just how much the body goes through during pregnancy and birth - especially a c-section. It experiences a lot of trauma.

Whats the answer? How can you get your pre-baby body back? Personally, I would just let your body rest and be for a few weeks. Think of all the stress, strain, excess weight it has had to carry, the stress on your joints and muscles not to mention the drugs pre and during birth. Our poor bodies!

As with anything that goes through a traumatic experience, it needs to recover.

Once you body has recovered that's when you start exercising and caring for it. Don't rush your body. It will let you know when it's ready.

Note: please don't ever prioritise how you look over your baby.

HOW DID I GET MY FIGURE BACK?

Honestly, it took me a good year to get it back. It wasn't easy; I had a good 3 and a bit stone (Approx 50 pounds) to lose.

I started doing the home workout (page 74) around 4 months after birth as I wanted to really make sure that my c-section was fully healed and ok. I was also terrified of trying to use my stomach muscles again. I tried to do the home workout 2-3 times a week. I weighed myself every 2 weeks and also measured my waist, hips, thighs and arms every Friday.

This home workout really kick started my new healthy living and I started to see very small results which motivated me even more to keep going. At around 6 months I took up pilates and started off at a very basic and beginner level. I attended a class once a week. I learnt a lot about my body and how the muscular system works whilst undertaking these pilates classes.

Along with the home workout which I did in an evening in between feeds, I also did a lot of walking during the daytime. This is such a brilliant way to shed those first few stubborn pounds. I walked to the shops, randomly around, to see friends and attend various mums groups. I was always on the go.

With time, my stomach muscles healed and became strong and toned along with the rest of my body. I completely changed my eating habits and diet to a much more carbohydrate restricted and more protein and vegetable fuelled diet. I also paid attention to my portion sizes and followed recipes for every meal.

Cutting out coffee and switching it for green tea also made a massive difference. In turn, this is all contributed to me losing my weight steadily but surely over the year. Still to this day I attend pilates once a week but now I have moved onto the advanced level - finally!

Shedding those first few pounds is tricky but once you start to see results and get your body used to exercising and eating well, the rest will come off with time.

DIET

I followed James Duigan on and off throughout my pregnancy and decided to pick up his Clean and Lean method again a few months ago. The great thing about his book is that it teaches you how to eat, portion sizes, understanding good fats and most importantly, how to ENJOY eating well. I now have all of his books and they are great but honestly, do take some getting used to. You have to completely re-think your eating habits and diet. Tough at first but then once you start to see results and notice an increase in your energy levels and a decrease in your waist size, you will happily stick to it!

Be careful of coffees loaded with milk - these are extremely fattening and should be avoided. If you need a caffeine fix, have a plain black coffee or if you must have milk, ask for a dash of milk on the side. I learnt this the hard way.

When I went out walking I would always grab a coffee en route - usually a large 'skinny' cappuccino or latte. For weeks, I couldn't understand why I wasn't losing as much weight as I thought I should be or noticing a difference in my figure, the answer was the coffee. Two to three of those a day will not help you lose the weight so be warned!

Alternatively, you can try switching from coffee to green tea. I know it is SO hard at first, but once you wean yourself off coffee, you will feel a lot better, notice a change in energy levels and you will also sleep more soundly too.

Even though I have tweaked my diet, I still allow myself cakes etc once in a while. I don't deprive myself of anything. I listen to my body. There are some days where I will crave salads and soups. Other days I will be heavily into my steak and vegetables, and then there are the days where I just need a pizza or a burger and fries!

Something I am very aware of though, and can now finally control is, my energy level. Eating bad food will make you feel tired and lethargic. Eating healthy food gives you energy. I need a lot of energy to run around after my son so I know if I eat a naughty meal I will feel sluggish and tired the next day and therefore unable to be as energetic as I'd like to be. Also, eating rubbish doesn't help me sleep particularly well. So there you go, even if I do want a naughty meal, my body automatically tells me that it's fine, but there are consequences the next day! I should really care about how fattening burgers etc are for me but truth be told, I'm more concerned about not sleeping well and feeling sluggish!!

So there you go, it is entirely possible to lose your excess baby weight through healthy eating, regular exercise and a healthy attitude whilst allowing yourself the occasional naughty treat.

I am extremely proud of how my body has changed. It isn't perfect but it is healthy, toned and strong.

BODILY CHANGES

You've had a baby. You now need to learn to accept your new body and the changes that go with it. Wider ribs? Wider hips? Podgy stomach? Varicose veins? I'm obviously not going to go into too much detail here - some things are best left unsaid! Every woman is different. Some women develop totally different bodies post-birth whereas some women hardly change at all.

Learn to accept and love your new body. It is what is - don't fight it. I now have wider ribs and shoulders from having a baby but my hips have shrunk - slightly odd but I have accepted it! There is nothing I can do to change that. I even have a varicose vein appearing on my calf. Short of getting surgery on it there is nothing I can do about it. I have a c-section scar across my lower abdomen which probably wont fade for another few years. All these things are reminders to me that I am a mother. I don't hate any of them. They make me proud.

"Confidence is sexy!"

STRETCH MARKS

Ugh! We spend so much time during pregnancy worrying about these wretched stripes - its almost inevitable that one or two will appear somewhere post birth. I remember covering myself in oil from my knees to my shoulders EVERYDAY when I was pregnant - my husband thought this was extreme behaviour at the time but now he understands why I took on such a drastic oiling regime for 9 months!

You can never fully get rid of stretch marks, they will always linger. The good news is they will get lighter over the years. Keep applying oil to them. If you are really concerned about them, there are laser treatments available to help zap them away. I still have one or two on my breasts which I have just accepted - I don't look at them in a negative way, more of a "I had a baby and this is what happens!".

SCARS

If you had a c-section, try rubbing on some coconut or rose hip oil twice a day - results are brilliant!

SKIN MAINTENANCE

Did you know that your skin is the largest organ you have!?

I recently discovered body brushing and it does wonders for the skin. It is a very quick and easy trick to help keen your skin looking bright and feeling smooth. Post birth, our skin can become really dry and flaky, body brushing is really great for combatting this.

BODY BRUSHING

What exactly is body brushing?

It's an exfoliating brush with natural boar bristles and massage nodules.

The buffing body brush can help with moving redundant skin cells and dirt which can clog the surface of your skin. Ensure you polish and massage all over to stimulate circulation, eliminate layers of dead skin and improve its overall appearance. The result? Smooth, radiant skin.

I am a massive fan of this. It may feel strange and a little painful when you first try it but you will soon become addicted to it, especially once you start to see the incredible results.

How to use the body brush?

✦ Start at the soles of your feet and work your way up the body using firm upward strokes towards the heart. Pay special attention to the backs of your thighs or areas where you have cellulite.

✦ When brushing your stomach and chest use clockwise sweeps.

✦ Apply just enough pressure so that it is stimulating enough to increase circulation but gentle on your skin. You should see a rosy flush to the areas you have brushed.

What does it do?

✦Gets rid of dead skin cells
✦Helps improve skins texture
✦Increases lymph circulation
✦Helps combat cellulite
✦Smooth away stretch marks.
✦Leaves radiant skin

Try and make a habit of body brushing in the morning before you shower. It's very easy and only takes 3 minutes.

Top Tip: Don't forget to moisturise your body each day. If you're feeling fancy before you go to bed, apply an oil.

"Treat the skin on your body with just as much care as you would for the skin on your face. Don't neglect it!"

FITNESS

By no means am I a fitness guru, but I have learnt a lot about my body and how to care for it since having a child; something I never really used to do pre children. Despite having a C-section, I have managed to get my figure back - it has taken me close to a year but I have managed it. I am strong, lean (with curves) and healthy. And yes, my arse still wobbles every now and then! I am human, not a bloody supermodel!

LOSING YOUR BABY WEIGHT

There is no right or wrong time limit in which to get your pre-baby body back. Do not compare yourself to other mums and please do not set yourself unrealistic goals. Be sensible about it and remember that every woman is different and some will lose it quicker than others. However you choose to lose it, do it healthily through sensible eating and exercise. Do not assume that you will lose it just through breastfeeding or stress! Do not starve yourself, skip meals or try exercising for 3 hours a day.

Losing weight should all be done sensibly and in moderation. Sleep and rest (where possible) is also fundamental.

Little Tip: cut out booze and processed sugar for a few weeks. You will notice a difference in energy levels.

Your body has been through a very traumatic experience. Let it recuperate before battering it. Be gentle with it. It needs time to heal from birth and recover from the drugs, hormones etc

CORE STRENGTH

It is so important to maintain a strong core, lower back and legs with an infant. The constant lifting, supporting and feeding positions really take their toll on your core and especially lower back. If the muscular strength isn't there to support these essential muscles then you could really damage yourself.

Strength becomes a necessity once your baby starts to get really heavy. I used to have terrible back pains from lifting my son awkwardly but now they have gone as my core is strong and my posture is better than it has ever been. Squatting each day has really helped to strengthen my lower back.

STRETCHING & POSTURE

I'll never forget being told after the birth of my son by one of the doctors - "remember your posture!" This was obviously the last thing on my mind. I couldn't even begin to think about sitting or standing, let alone standing up straight!

As I mentioned at the start of this book, as I had an emergency c-section it has been so important for me to sit tall and stand straight on a daily basis. Not only has it helped my back from where it was especially weak post surgery but also has done immense wonders for my core from the cesarian. It is such a simple thing to do but one of the hardest things to remember to do. I never used to have good posture. After I had my son, I noticed my spine was slightly 'S' shaped from carrying the weight from pregnancy. Having seen my S posture in the mirror, I wanted to do as much as I could for my back and my posture.

As soon as you are given the all clear to exercise (usually around 8-12 weeks), I would definitely recommend some regular light stretching. Whilst it may not seem like much of a workout, nor is it supposed to, it will help stretch out your muscles, relieve tension and stress and help your blood circulation around your body. If that isn't enough, it will help to relax your mind. Be gentle though and don't over do it - especially if you have had a c-section or complicated birth.

"When walking around, even if at home, contract your stomach muscles."

The main areas that are affected in the early days of motherhood are lower back (from picking up), core (from lack of muscle strength & tone), shoulders (from feeding in various positions and carrying) and neck (mostly from feeding and staring down at your baby)!

Important rules to remember when bending down:

- ✦Always use & bend your legs.
- ✦Never use just your back.
- ✦Don't twist your back - adjust your feet and legs accordingly
- ✦Never try to balance on one foot/leg when picking something up - have a fixed two feet position.
- ✦Engage your core when lifting.

If you have had a c-section, be careful not to do too much stretching involving arms over head and please obtain your doctor's approval before conducting any form of exercise.

"Always bend the legs when picking up."

WORKOUTS

Remember the Cindy Crawford VHS?! Anyone fancy a Jane Fonda workout? I am joking! Home workouts have (luckily) advanced since those days. Whilst Cindy's and Jane's exercise methods worked back then, they were also very long!

I'm a big fan of "at home" workouts as I'm not a fan of working out in front of others, and I am always on the hunt for new exercises and workouts to do in the comfort of my own home. What's not to love about that?!

Home workouts can be short and sweet. They don't need to be a gruelling 60 minute workout in order to see results; although they do exist!

We need to accept that we are not going to see immediate results. Exercising and eating well over the space of a few weeks will lead to noticeable results but it takes time, discipline and patience.

When you start your fitness journey, try to weigh yourself at the same time each week and measure your hips, thighs, waist and arms each week too. This is a great way to monitor your progress and notice the changes.

Exercising at home doesn't mean you can't get creative. There are a few workouts available through itunes such as Ballet Beautiful, Tracy Anderson, Yoga Studio, 7min Workout, various fitness apps and several other workout options online. Don't be afraid to switch it up every now and then to avoid getting bored.

Find a workout style that suits you and build up from there. It could be a walk, run, set of exercises each day, workout video on TV, yoga, swimming, pilates or going to the gym.

"Squatting, lunging and planking - try to do these everyday."

Here is a great "at home" workout. All you need is an exercise/yoga mat, bottle of water and a timer (which most phones now have).

Do 30 seconds of each exercise with a 1 minute break between each set. Do 3 sets 3-5 times a week.

- Jumping jacks
- Squats with weights
- Plank
- Side plank with weights
- Push ups toes and knees
- Crunches
- Squat jumps
- Bridges
- High knees
- Lunges with weights

If you are unsure of what each exercise looks like, either google it or you tube it - much easier than me trying to draw a diagram or explain to you!

ALWAYS...

Listen to your body. Always check with your doctor before you undertake any form of exercise, even if its stretching. If you have had a c-section, or complicated natural birth, please make sure you wait the allocated amount of time before resuming exercise. Whilst your stitches may look healed externally, internally is a whole different matter. You do not want to risk tearing those.

SOCIAL MEDIA

Nothing annoys me quite as much as celebrities who boast on Instagram or other forms of social media about how they are back to their pre baby body only 5 weeks after giving birth. This just sets such an unrealistic guide for normal mothers who don't have a live-in chef, nutritionist, personal trainer, masseuse, nanny, housekeeper, maid etc. My advice, ignore them! Focus on accepting your new body, adapt a healthy diet and lifestyle and slowly start to build up your weekly exercise routine.

Be wary of 'fitness' videos on social media too. Many of the videos you see will be of people effortlessly doing a plank, or a complex yoga move, or upside down something or other - do not try this at home!

Try & avoid it at all costs!

BODY SHAPES

Some women can really lose all sense of style and fashion choices once a small person enters their world. Just because you have a child doesn't mean you need to dress like a school matron or adopt the whole 'curtain' look. You can still wear skinny jeans, an LBD, heels or a backless number!

So you have a new figure post baby - how do you know what shape you are and how do you dress that shape?!

In order to dress according to your shape, you first need to know and understand your body shape. It's amazing how many women don't know their shape. Always dress according to your body shape.

Let's have a look at the different body shapes:

◆ Straight

The bust and hips are basically the same size. The waist is slightly smaller than the bust and hips.

How to dress?

The key to dressing a straight body type is to dress proportionally the top and bottom of your body while enhancing your waist. To create a more curvaceous effect, add volume proportionally to your upper and lower body by mixing and matching suggested separates.

Look for tops that will add curves to your upper half and create a more defined waist:

- Tops with nipped or belted waists.
- Off the shoulder, boat-neck tops, wide V or U necks.
- Structured shoulders or flutter sleeves.
- Embellishments around the bust and shoulders.
- Tops that are full, rushed or flowing around the bust.

◆ Pear

The hips are larger than the bust, and the waist gradually slopes out to the hips.

How to dress?

The key to dressing a pear body type is to enhance and add volume to your upper body while emphasising your waist and de-emphasizing your lower body to create a balanced, hourglass appearance.

When dressing a pear body type, look for tops that will will help balance your lower half while accentuating your defined waist:

- Tops with nipped or fitted waists.
- Off the shoulder, boat-neck tops, wide V or U necks.
- Structured shoulders or flutter sleeves.
- Embellishments around the bust and shoulders.
- Bright colours and bold patterns.

◆ Spoon

The hips are larger than the bust and the hips have a "shelf" appearance. The waist is slightly smaller than the bust.

How to dress?

The key to dressing a spoon body type is to draw attention to your upper body while de-emphasizing your tummy and hips to create a more balanced appearance and create the illusion of an hourglass figure. Your legs are one of your best assets, so feel free to play with skirt lengths and show them off!

Look for tops that will help balance your lower half while accentuating your defined waist and camouflaging any tummy bulges:

- Tops with empire waists.
- Off the shoulder, boat-neck tops, wide V or U necks.
- Tops with rouching or embellishments around the bust.
- Tops that skim your midsection without adding volume.

- Strapless tops that show off your shoulders.

✦ Hourglass

The bust and hips are basically the same size and your waist is well defined.

How to dress?

The key to dressing an hourglass body type is to proportionally dress the top and bottom of your body while accentuating your waist.

Look for tops that will accentuate your waist and maintain the balanced look of your figure. Look for:

- Belted tops.
- Tops with banding or nipping at the waist.
- Form-fitting tops.
- Wrap-style tops.
- Tailored shirts and jackets.

✦ Inverted Triangle

The bust is large, the hips are narrow and the waist is not very well defined

How to dress?

The key to dressing an inverted triangle body type is to balance your broader shoulders, chest and back with your narrower lower body to create more of an hourglass effect. This is achieved by choosing clothes that add curves to your hips and bottom while creating a more defined waist.

Look for tops that will accentuate your waist and help balance your bust with your hips. Look for:

- Narrow v-necks.
- Tops with banding or nipping at the waist.
- Wrap-style tops.
- Tailored shirts and jackets.
- Dark coloured tops.

RETAIL THERAPY

WAIT!! Do not go shopping for new clothes a week after giving birth! Wait until your bloating has gone down, your hormones are back to normal, you've lost a little weight and all scars are healed. Wait around 12 weeks. Any sooner and it will depress you. Clothes won't fit, you won't feel good about yourself and the whole trip will be a disaster. Again, do not buy a whole new wardrobe as your body will change in size yet again as time goes on and you lose more weight. Only buy the basics such as underwear, jeans and basic tops for now.

Think loose and comfy clothing post birth. Dress your shape. We all see clothes and think "that's gorgeous!" but our inner fashion conscience is screaming "that won't work on this figure!" Be smart with your fashion choices. Trying to struggle into the wrong outfit can damage your confidence as much as it can damage yourself trying to get it on!

Spend some time on shopping for YOU. Once a child arrives into our lives, we mostly think about them... this includes shopping! Your automatic thoughts whilst shopping would be to your kids and what they might need. Don't think about your little ones... think about you and what you need and/or fancy in your wardrobe. Switch off and enjoy the retail THERAPY!!

UNDERWEAR

I feel like I need to briefly (pardon the pun) flag this up as it's pretty important and I very nearly fell victim to wearing maternity underwear forever!

I had to wear those really high waisted pants (M&S specials) after delivery to avoid catching my c-section scar. These were horrific and as soon as I didn't have to wear them anymore, I tossed every single pair straight in the bin. Ugh.

My boobs shrunk after breastfeeding, a common problem but I just accepted it.

I've never been large in the chest department so its not something that really matters to me.

In turn, I had to buy a whole new set of bras - in white, tan, cream and black. These are the everyday bras - t-shirt bras. nothing fancy about them, just practical and do what I need them to do. I also bought new panties, thongs etc. These are all great and mothball free but they aren't SEXY.

It didn't even cross my mind that my underwear was as plain as the walls in a hospital! I realised soon enough that my poor husband had been looking at the most boring underwear ever. Now, he didn't expect me to get all Agent Provocateur in his face, but surely I could do better than M&S basics!

I bought a couple of pretty and sexy lingerie sets that didn't break the bank and also didn't scream SLUT MUMMY! I found a happy medium - thank goodness.

Since then, my body has changed again due to weight loss so I have had to overhaul my undies collection again. It's not the end of the world though is it, I mean, a woman can never have enough underwear.

Bottom line (see what I did there!?) is try not to neglect your sexy side... it is so easy to do so with a child in your life, but try to make an effort every now and then.

"Don't forget your ooh la la!"

3
MIND

"Positive mind, positive vibes, positive life."

MIND

The mind is such a delicate part of our body. It controls everything we do, who we are as a person and every action we take.

Having a baby can cause absolute havoc on your mind's chemistry. The lack of sleep, intense stimulation, huge responsibility and irregular timings can have a severe effect on your mental well-being.

You will question yourself a lot in the early days. Is any of this normal? How should I be feeling? Am I doing this right? What if something happens? How do I do this?

It's normal - everything you're experiencing and feeling is normal. Most women go through exactly the same. I nearly lost my mind and the plot on several occasions during the first few weeks after giving birth.

It gets worse before it gets better - just keep this in mind and it won't be as much of a shock when you do go through a tough patch in the early days.

Try to enjoy it, it goes so quickly. There will be great days, mediocre days and well and truly sh*t days. You have to take it as it comes. Try to see the best in every situation and enjoy these moments.

I really struggled in my first few months as I was away from my family and on the other side of the world. I look back on it now and whilst it was extremely tough and I felt very alone at times, I have lots of happy memories.

Someone asked me recently how I would describe motherhood - my answer was this:

✦ Motherhood is similar to a computer screen whereby you have hundreds of windows open at the same time. You are constantly thinking about things that need doing, remembering to do stuff, appointments, play dates, food times, etc. You are always on the go.

✦ As a mother, it is overwhelming how much stuff you have on your mind all the time. It is very hard to switch off but we all need to switch off when possible otherwise we will go mad or have a meltdown.

As a mother, it is very normal to feel mentally and physically exhausted. It is the most demanding job out there. You are on call 24/7 with very little time off. Whilst it may be an incredibly demanding and at times difficult role, it is also the most rewarding. Try not to forget that.

It's normal not always to enjoy every single day of being a Mother - some days are much harder and more trying than others.

Through all the bad days, remember that there is light at the end of the tunnel. Speak to other mums and you'll realise just how normal it is to be feeling how you do, experiencing all the same things as other mothers.

"You are not alone, there are thousands of other mothers in exactly the same boat as you."

SUPPORT NETWORK & COMMUNICATION

It is really important to have a good support network around you. Talk to those around you; family, friends and other mothers you have met throughout your pregnancy journey. We all have good and bad days - **fact**. It's so useful & comforting knowing that we all have people we can contact and reach out to when we are having a wobble or a bad day. There are lots of wobbles during the first few weeks and months of having a baby so make sure you talk to those around you - they aren't there to judge you, they are there to listen, comfort and let you rant. It is better to talk about a problem and have a good rant rather than bottle it all up. This will only lead to a build up of frustration in due course, which you want to avoid at all costs.

I didn't believe in needing to talk to others, I thought I was super human and didn't need to rant. How wrong I was. I cannot imagine not being able to compare notes with other fellow mothers whom I have met along the way, rant about the frustrations of motherhood and if nothing else, know that I am not alone in thinking and feeling how I do. Those around you will not judge you, they will help you. Don't ever be afraid to utilise the support of friends and family around you.

Talk to other mothers. This is great for asking advice, discussing problems and comparing notes. Very therapeutic for new mums. Especially if you're all new to this, it really helps knowing that you're not going mad and you're not alone. It's healthy and useful to hear other stories, experiences and it will help you with yours.

And finally, remember to reciprocate as the other mothers around you need you as much as you need them.

"A problem shared is a problem halved."

HOW TO NOT LOSE YOUR SH*T

It is very easy to flip out as a new mum. Expect a rough couple of weeks in the early days - sleep deprivation will bring the worst out of you and your partner.

It is perfectly normal to reach the edge of despair and feel totally hopeless at some point during the early stages of motherhood.

Don't be too harsh on yourself - you're new to this. There is no right or wrong, the majority of motherhood is trial and error.

Losing your temper and getting frustrated are very common. Every time you can feel yourself bubbling up, count to 10. Walk out of the room and take a few deep breaths, then go back in. It is amazing how a tiny little human being can wind you up and push buttons you never knew you had. Remember how vulnerable and dependent that little person is on you. They can't really communicate with you just yet so try and be patient and remember that they are probably just as frustrated as you.

Next time you are getting frustrated about something, whether it be feeding, sleeping or changing a nappy, try the following before you reach boiling point!

✦Take 3 deep breaths.

✦Count to 10.

✦Stretch.

✦Have a warm drink.

✦Talk about it.

✦Hug it out.

BOREDOM

Doing the same thing day in, day out can become very monotonous, tedious and actually dangerous.

When you feel comfortable enough to do so, try switching up your weekly routine. Plan out what you are going to do that week. Don't set yourself an unrealistic schedule, otherwise you will frustrate yourself and tire yourself and the baby out. Do an activity a day - whether that is going for a coffee one day, and a sing a long group the next. Not only will it get you out of the house but it will also get you talking to others. It is also an opportunity for your little one to mingle with other babies and explore being social.

It is important to maintain the baby's routine so make sure you slot things in and around that. Still to this day I try not to break my son's routine and base everything around it. Most days I will try and go for a walk with a friend and grab a juice for an hour, or go for a swim, playgroup, playdates etc... Then one day during the week, I make no plans. I chill with my son and we stay at home, watch a film, cook, play and tickle.

I find this works because I have spent the other days out and about. I'm not bored and my son isn't bored.

It's so easy to forget that your child needs to socialise with other children as part of their social development. This means that you need to get out there and also mingle with other mothers so you can sort out play dates etc. This motherhood malarky isn't for the socially inept!

"Happy Mummy, Happy Baby!"

BABY BRAIN

We have all heard of the dreaded 'baby brain'. Yes, our change in brain chemistry means our reasoning slows down a bit during pregnancy and post birth. Don't worry though, once the sleep deprivation passes, there are ways you can stimulate your brain again and try to get it going. I found that doing a little reading each day helped me to switch back on.

I tried to read the news whenever I could, it is quite handy to know what is going on outside of your baby world! When my son started sleeping through and I didn't have to do a dream feed, I started reading books before bed.

Obviously, some nights I would just crawl into bed and sleep! Now though, I make much more of an effort to read. I find it helps me to switch off and wind down before bed. Also, try to make an effort not always to talk about baby stuff with your friends and partner. Engage in adult chat once in a while. It helps!

YOUR SPACE

It's really important to have your time away from the baby. Take up a hobby and try to get out of the house once a week without the baby for some time and space alone. It does wonders and also means you have that time to look forward to each week. Everyone needs some time out now and then. It is perfectly normal.

This is your time to enjoy doing whatever it is that you like to do - something that helps you switch off, unwind or distract you. It is only healthy for you to have some time to yourself so spend it how you want.

At first, it's hard to leave the little one and go and enjoy yourself without feeling guilty. It took me weeks to be able to actually go and do something for myself without feeling terrible that I had left my baby with my husband. I felt like a bad mother for not being there 24/7. With time though, I was able to go and enjoy myself without feeling bad but knowing that my husband was also more than happy to spend some alone time with our son. I'm not saying you need to go off for the whole day but do try and head out for a couple of hours. Try going out for 30 mins to start off with then build up from there.

"Never judge a fellow mother, always support each other."

A FEW FINAL WORDS

I really hope this book has been of some use to you, and put a smile on your face along the way. As I said at the beginning, I am a first time mum who has experienced everything you have read in this book over the last 14 months. Trial and error - that's what it is all about; motherhood, life, fashion choices, hair styles - all trial and error. Eventually though, we get it right!

A lot of the content of this book is logical or common sense but it is really amazing how baby brain (and hormones!) can get the better of us and we find ourselves choosing ridiculous clothes, hairstyles or lipstick colours. Sometimes you just need to hear it from someone else to realise that there is a different and perhaps easier (more effective/less humiliating) way of doing something.

Next time you are feeling a little run down in the beauty department, whack on a face mask, light a candle and have a hot bath. Remember, to always make time for yourself and your pampering - routine for your baby, routine for you too!

And don't forget to add a little make up before you leave the house - let's give all those mums-to-be out there hope that we can all feel great and look radiantly happy!

Remember you have a beautiful baby, try and enjoy this precious time as much as possible because before you know it, they will have grown up and be attending school! Take the good days with the bad and please never take any of it for granted. Even when you don't feel it, you are incredibly lucky to have been chosen to be a mother.

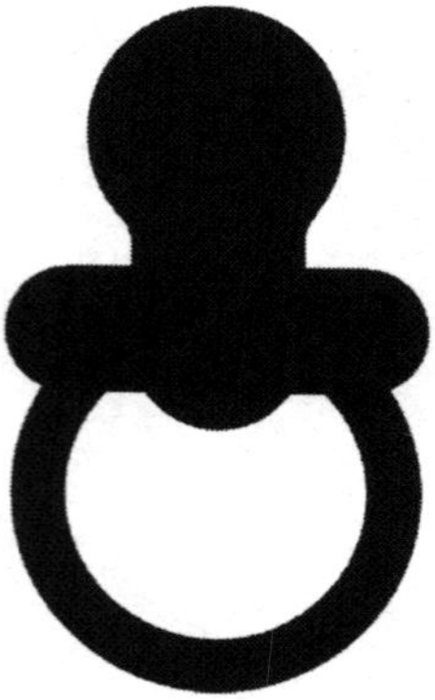

THANK YOUS

I owe massive thanks to my husband for his patience and listening throughout this whole writing process. Thank you for letting me warble on about the size of my arse and boobs. Thanks for still fancying me too! x

To my son for sleeping when he is supposed to so I could write this book!

I love you both more than words. x

To Moots for teaching me everything I needed to know about a baby and for your endless support. Oh and for making sure I don't leave the house looking revolting! x

To all my family & friends who contributed to this book and for their criticism and pointers. I won't threaten to thank you with my cooking... x

The moment a child is born, the mother is also born. She never existed before. The woman existed, but the mother never did. A mother is something absolutely new.

Baby & A Blonde
A Modern Mother's Journey